Life Stories
Guy Fawkes

Clare Chandler

Illustrated by Barbara Loftus

HODDER
Wayland

an imprint of Hodder Children's Books

Life Stories

Louis Braille
Christopher Columbus
Grace Darling
Guy Fawkes
Anne Frank
Gandhi
Helen Keller
Martin Luther King
Nelson Mandela
Florence Nightingale
Shakespeare
Mother Teresa

Cover and title page: A portrait of Guy Fawkes as a young man.

Editor: Polly Goodman
Designer: Joyce Chester

First published in Great Britain in 1995 by Wayland (Publishers) Ltd
Reprinted in 2000 by Hodder Wayland, an imprint of Hodder Children's Books

© Hodder Wayland 1995

Hodder Children's Books, a division of Hodder Headline,
338 Euston Road, London NW1 3BH

British Library Cataloguing in Publication Data
Chandler, Clare
Guy Fawkes. – (Life Stories)
I. Title II. Loftus, Barbara III. Series
942. 055092

ISBN 0 7502 2300 6

Typeset by Joyce Chester, England
Printed and bound in Italy by G. Canale & C.S.p.A., Turin

Contents

Words in **bold** are explained in the glossary on page 30.

5 November, 1605

The cathedral clock had just struck midnight. It was cold and damp in the cellar, which was lit by the sputtering light of a single candle. A rat scuttled past. Guy shivered. Next to him, in wooden barrels, was the gunpowder which was to blow up the **Houses of Parliament**. The cellar was right below the Houses of Parliament, where King James I and all his lords were going to meet the next day. Guy hoped to get rid of them all with one big blast.

Then he heard a noise. Footsteps. Men's voices. A key turned in the lock of the door. Swinging a lantern in front of them, in walked the King's Guard...

Why did Guy Fawkes want to blow up the Houses of Parliament? To answer that question we will have to look at his life story.

This was Parliament in the time of King James I.

Growing up

Guy was born in York in 1570. Sadly, his father died when Guy was only nine years old. His mother married again and went to live with her new husband in a village near York. Guy was sent to boarding school, but he still spent his holidays with his mother, two sisters and his stepfather.

Some people think that Guy Fawkes was born in this house in York. It is now a hotel.

Unlike his father, Guy's stepfather was a member of the **Catholic Church**. To be a **Catholic** in those days was dangerous, because King James I and the English Church were **Protestant**. They wanted everyone in England to be Protestant. King James made life very hard for Catholics. They had to **worship** at home in secret. If they were found out, they were put in prison, or made to pay huge **fines**.

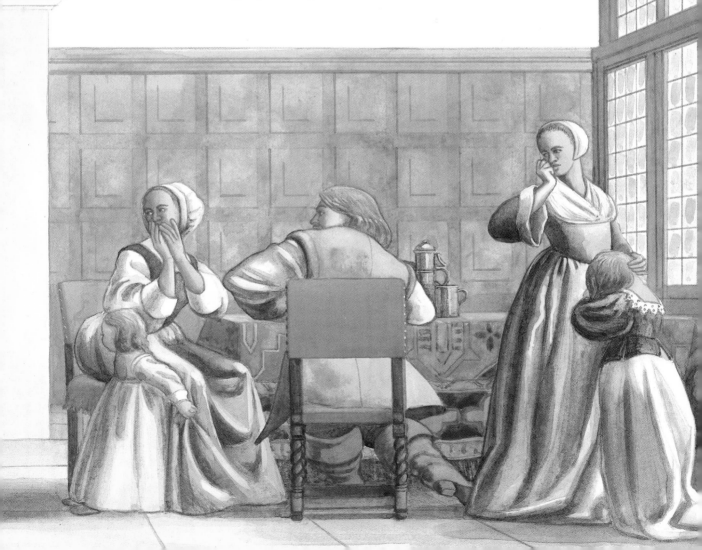

Catholics' houses often had a priest-hole, which was a small room or a cupboard where the priest could hide if anyone came. If the priest was caught by Protestant officials, he was **executed**.

A Catholic priest is executed. Father Garnet was accused of being involved in the Gunpowder Plot.

Many of Guy's school friends were Catholics as well. He admired the way they stood up for what they believed. So when he was a young man, Guy decided to become a Catholic himself.

Catholic churches all over Europe, like this one in France, were wrecked and anything of value taken.

A soldier abroad

On his twenty-first birthday, Guy **inherited** some land from his father. Soon afterwards, he sold everything to go and become a soldier in the Low Countries, the area that is now Holland and Belgium. For seven years, Guy fought for the army of the Catholic Spanish king, Philip.

The Spanish army had to attack many **fortified towns**. The only way to get into the towns was by breaking down the walls which surrounded them. A barrel of gunpowder was put in a crack in the wall, a long trail of gunpowder was trickled away from it, and the end was lit. The explosion made a hole in

Guy Fawkes as a young man.

10

the wall that the soldiers could enter.
Guy became an expert at using
gunpowder, and he was made a
captain in the army.

Riding to Spain

While Guy was in the Low Countries, he kept in touch with some of his friends in England. Many of them had become poor because of the fines they had to pay for not belonging to the **Protestant Church**. Others had been put in prison.

King Philip II of Spain fought for Catholics all over Europe.

Guy's friend, Thomas Wintour, was going to see King Philip of Spain to ask him to help the English Catholics. Guy decided to go with him. They set off together for the long journey on horseback across France and the mountains of Spain to Madrid. They hoped that King Philip might send an army against King James I, or at least ask the English king not to be so harsh with his Catholic subjects.

Catholics are dragged from their houses by soldiers of the Protestant king, James I. In the upstairs window you can see they have caught a priest holding a mass.

However, King Philip said he could not help, and they had to set off, bitterly disappointed, on the long journey back. It took them weeks to get home and as they rode, Wintour told Guy about a secret plan. A group of Catholics was plotting to kill James I and his **Parliament**.

Guy already knew some of the plotters. He had been at school with the two Wright brothers, and Thomas Percy was a neighbour from Yorkshire. Wintour explained that they needed Guy to help because of his knowledge of gunpowder. Guy eventually agreed to help and he returned to England for his first meeting with his fellow **conspirators** in the Gunpowder Plot.

The plot

The leader of the plot was Robert Catesby, a handsome and popular young man. He thought that if the plotters could get rid of King James I and most of the ruling lords, then the Catholics would be able to rise up and take power. When the plotters met together to discuss the plan, he made them all swear an **oath of secrecy**.

Catesby's plan was to dig a tunnel under the Lords' Chamber in the Houses of Parliament. The plotters would fill it with gunpowder. Then, when the lords were meeting there, they would blow it up. The first step was to **rent** the house next door to the Lords' Chamber. Then Guy moved into the house pretending to be the caretaker. Instead of his real name, Guy called himself John Johnson.

King James I was not well-loved by his people. They thought that he was ugly and that his tongue was too big for his mouth.

The digging began. Altogether, there were thirteen conspirators, and they all took it in turns to dig through to the Parliament building. It was backbreaking work. First, they had to make a hole in the brick wall of the cellar. Then they had to tunnel through the earth, before digging through the stone **foundations** of the Lords' Chamber, which were nearly 3 metres thick.

This cartoon shows Guy Fawkes being watched by the eye of God.

The men had been digging for several weeks when suddenly, they heard a strange loud noise above their heads. Guy went to have a look. He found that there was a cellar under the Lords' Chamber which had been used by a coal merchant. The coal merchant was moving out. The conspirators had no need to dig after all! So they rented the cellar and put the thirty-six barrels of gunpowder in it, hidden under a pile of firewood.

Caught red-handed

On the night of 4 November, everything was in place beneath the Lords' Chamber. Guy was waiting beside the barrels of gunpowder with only the touchpaper to light. Suddenly, the King's Guard walked in!

Someone had written a letter to one of the Catholic lords, Lord Monteagle, warning him not to attend Parliament on 5 November. The **anonymous letter** said that Parliament would receive 'a terrible blow' on that day. For his own safety, Lord Monteagle should go to the country.

The letter which was sent to Lord Monteagle. The lords never found out who sent it.

Lord Monteagle took the letter straight to another lord, who showed it to the king. King James, whose father had been blown up by gunpowder, guessed what the letter meant immediately. He ordered a search of the rooms below the Lords' Chamber.

Guy Fawkes and the gunpowder were found. When the guards arrested Guy he tried to fight them off. But they were too strong for him. They dragged him to the king's chamber and questioned him in front of King James.

Guy Fawkes is arrested.

Even when he was questioned by the king, Guy did not say he was sorry. He said that if he had not been found, he would have set light to the gunpowder and blown up the king and his lords. In the next two days, the rest of the plotters were either killed, or caught and put in the **Tower of London**.

Thomas Percy and Robert Catesby, two of the conspirators, are killed by the king's soldiers.

In the Tower of London

For a long time after he was caught, Guy insisted that his name was John Johnson, and he would not give the names of his fellow conspirators. He was put in an underground cell next to the torture chamber. After three days of questioning, Guy still refused to name the others, so the torture began.

Guy was put on the **rack** with his hands tied above his head and with ropes bound around his ankles. Then the ropes were pulled tighter and tighter. After two days of this terrible torture, Guy gave the names of all the conspirators.

After days of torture, Guy finally signs his confession.

Guy's signatures before and after being tortured.

Execution

Guy Fawkes and the other conspirators were tried and found guilty of **treason**. The punishment for treason in those days was a very nasty death. The traitors were to be hung, drawn and quartered. First they were dragged through the jeering crowds to the place of execution.

The executioner pulls out the heart from one of the conspirators who has been hung and cut up.

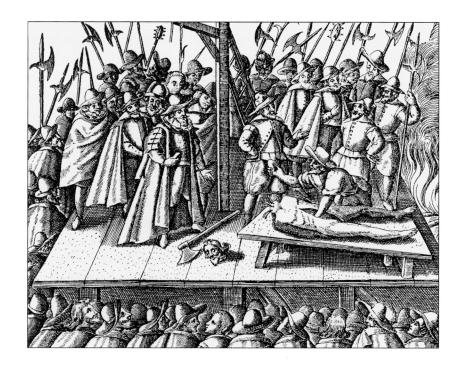

They were hung by their necks, cut down while they were still alive, and cut into pieces. Then their heads were stuck on spikes in the centre of London. This was done as a warning to anyone else who thought of plotting against the king.

The plotters' heads were cut off and left on stakes in the centre of London.

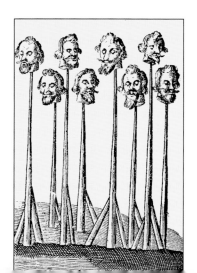

On the night of 5 November, the king's supporters celebrated the failure of the Gunpowder Plot. They lit bonfires and made a model of Guy Fawkes out of straw. Then they threw the straw model on to the fire.

Today, people in Britain still celebrate the failure of the plot. Every year, on the evening of 5 November, people have parties around a bonfire. And on the top of every bonfire is a 'Guy' – a figure that represents Guy Fawkes.

The air is filled with the flashes, bangs and the smoke of fireworks exploding. These remind people of what would have happened to Parliament if Guy Fawkes and the gunpowder had not been found.

On 5 November every year, a 'Guy' is still burned on top of bonfires all over Britain.

Glossary

Anonymous letter A letter that is not signed by the person who wrote it.

Catholic A person who is a member of the Catholic Church.

Catholic Church The Christian Church ruled by the Pope in Rome, Italy.

Conspirators Plotters.

Executed Killed as a punishment.

Fines Money paid as punishments.

Fortified towns Towns surrounded by walls to defend them from attack.

Foundations The underground walls of a building.

Houses of Parliament The buildings in London where Parliament meets.

Inherited Received as an heir.

Oath of secrecy A serious promise to keep something secret.

Parliament The group of people in Britain who make the laws of the country.

Protestant A person who is a member of the Protestant Church.

Protestant Church The church which broke away from the Catholic Church in the 1500s and is no longer ruled by the Pope.

Rack A machine used for torturing people which stretched their bodies.

Rent To pay money to use a house.

Touchpaper A length of string which is attached to gunpowder and lit in order to make the gunpowder explode.

Tower of London A building in London which was used as a prison. It is now a museum.

Treason To plot against or harm the ruler of your country.

Worship To pray.

Date chart

1570 Guy Fawkes is born in York, England.

1579 Guy's father, Edward Fawkes dies.

1581 Guy's mother marries a Catholic, Denis Bainbridge.

1587 Mary Queen of Scots, a Catholic, is executed.

1591 Guy inherits his father's estate.

1592 Guy sells his estate and goes to the Low Countries to fight for the Spanish king.

1596 Siege of Calais. Guy shows such bravery that he is given command of a company.

1603 Queen Elizabeth I dies. James I becomes King of England.

Guy travels to Spain with Thomas Wintour to plead with King Philip of Spain on behalf of English Catholics.

1604 Guy returns to England. The conspirators rent the house next to the Lords' Chamber in the Houses of Parliament and begin digging.

1605 5 November
Just after midnight, Guy Fawkes and the gunpowder are discovered by the King's Guard.
Following Guy's arrest, the rest of the conspirators are killed or imprisoned.

1606 30–31 January
The conspirators are executed.

Books to read

Bonfire Night by Clare Chandler (Wayland, 1997)
Stuarts: Craft Topics, by Rachel Wright (Watts, 1993)
The Stuarts by Andrew Langley (Hamlyn, 1993)

Tudors and Stuarts by Peggy Burns (Wayland, 1994)
What Do We Know About the Tudors and Stuarts by Richard Tames (Simon and Schuster, 1994)

Index

Picture acknowledgements
The publishers would like to thank the
following for allowing their photographs to be
used in this book: British Library, London/
Bridgeman Art Library 9 (top); Mary Evans
Picture Library *Cover, Title page,* 9 (bottom), 10,
13, 15, 20–21, 23, 24, 27;
National Portrait Gallery 13 (top); Prado,
Madrid/Bridgeman Art Library, London 16;
Topham Picture Source 4, 25, 29; Wayland
Picture Library 18, 22; York & County Press 6.